PLAYING WITH PLANS

Michael Storm

Here are all sorts of houses.

I like this little house best.

I give a picture of the house
to Mr. Jones the builder.
"Please build me a house like that,
Mr. Jones," I say.
But—

4

The picture is very small.
And—

we cannot live in our house
if Mr. Jones builds it as small as
it looks in the picture.

Mr. Jones cannot build our house
if we give him a picture.

Instead, we must give him—

special drawings, like these.

One centimetre on these drawings
stands for one metre on the wall
of our house.

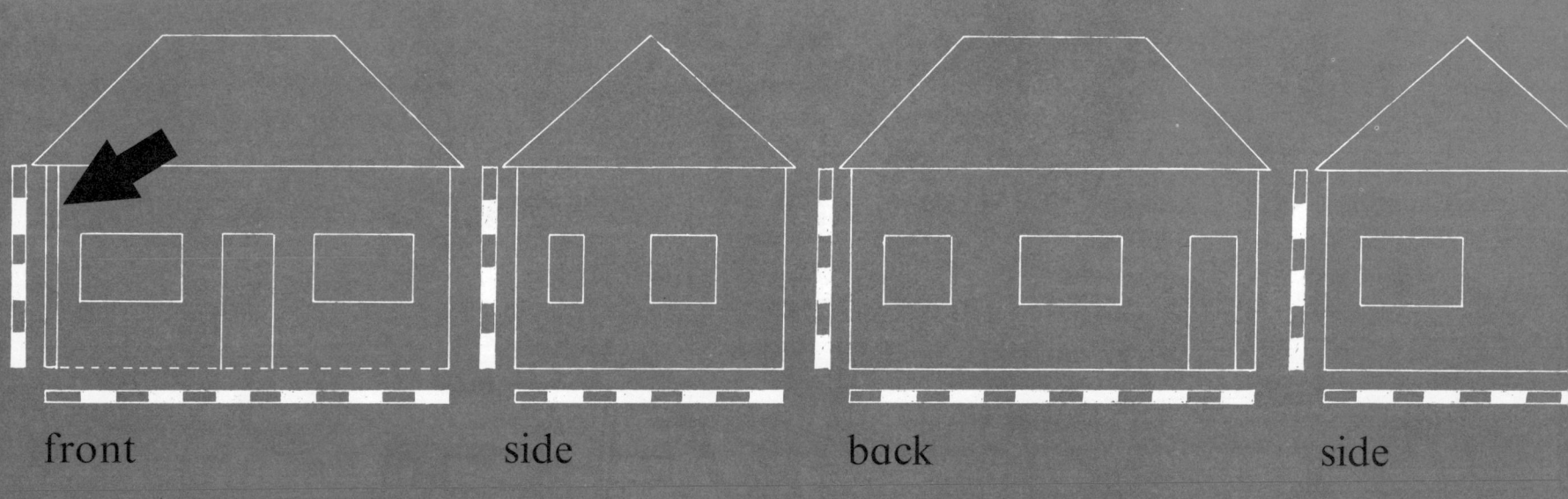

front   side   back   side

0   1 metre

These are called **scale drawings.**
Now Mr. Jones can tell
how big we want our house.

The front wall (dotted line)
is six centimetres long.

But one centimetre on the drawing
stands for one metre on the wall.

Mr. Jones makes the wall
six metres long.

Measure the double line.
How high do we want the wall?

Now Mr. Jones can tell how
many doors and windows we want.

We could not show them all
in the picture.

How many windows in the back wall?

At last our house is built.

Mr Jones Builder

NO 153

But—

there are no rooms in our house!
What went wrong?
Is it the builder's fault?

No, because our scale drawings
did not show him the rooms
we wanted inside.
For this, Mr. Jones needs—

a plan.

key to plan

0   1 metre

Two centimetres
stand for one metre.

window

door

path

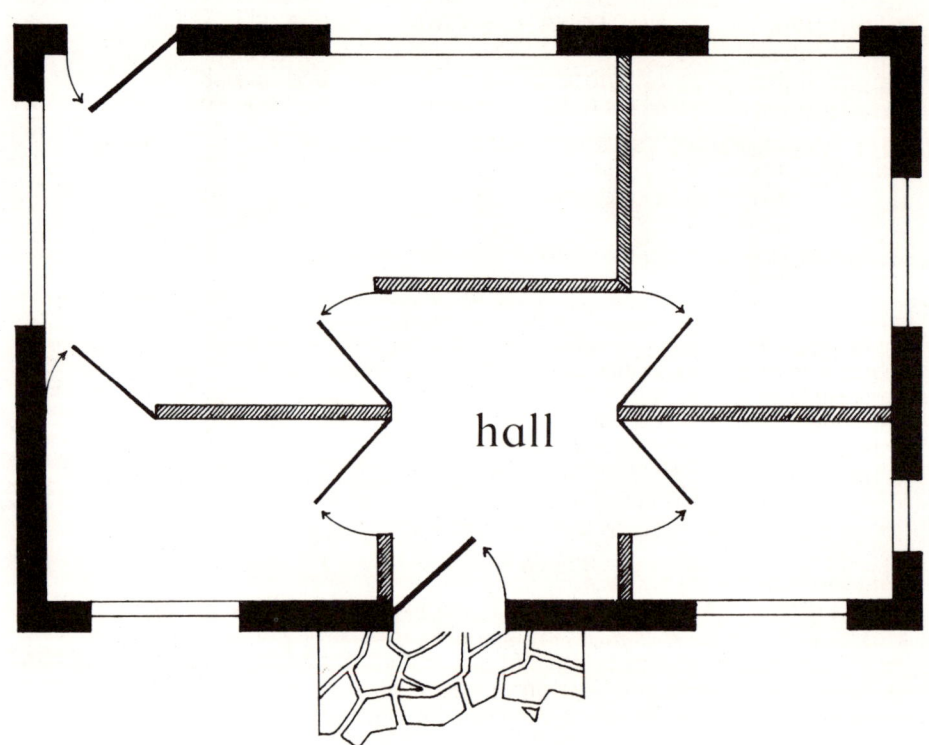

hall

Now we can see the rooms
inside our house.

How many rooms are there?

Can you find the front door?

How wide is the hall?

On the plan,
the windows look like this

and the doors look like this

What does this stand for?
Page 12 will remind you.

But our house still is not ready to live in.
We have no furniture to put in the rooms.

Wait a minute—

here it comes now!
But how are we going to arrange
the furniture inside the house?

What we need is—

another plan.

key to plan

0   1 metre
Two centimetres
stand for one metre.

window		path		
sink		door		
cooker		bath		
television		basin		
round table		settee		
armchair		chair		
lavatory		bed		

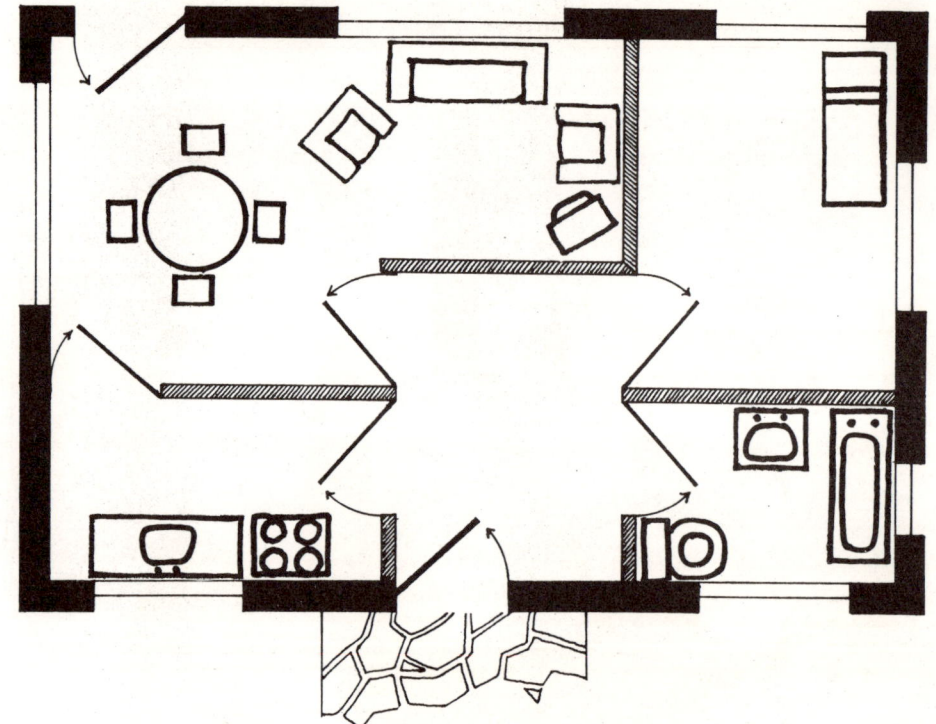

We have put in chairs, a table, a bed, and a settee. Look at the plan.
Can you see where we have put them?

Where are the men going to put these two things?

At last the new house is ready.

key to plan

0   1 metre
Two centimetres
stand for one metre.

- ▬ window
- ⊡ sink
- cooker
- ▭ television
- ◯ round table
- ▯ armchair
- lavatory
- path
- door
- bath
- basin
- settee
- ▫ chair
- bed

- (M) Mary
- (A) Andrew
- (S) Sally
- (P) Peter
- (J) Jim
- (F) Flash

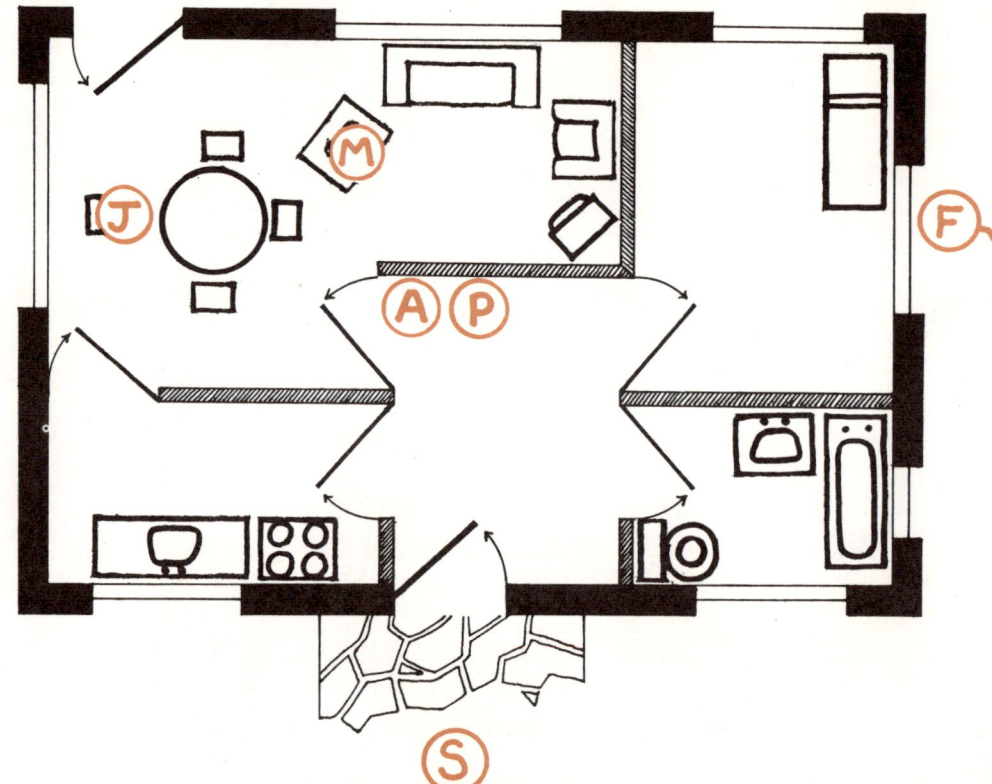

Look at the children.

Mary is watching the television.
Where is Jim?

Are there enough chairs
for everyone?

Andrew and Peter have
taken their coats off in the hall.

But where is Sally?
Look for her on the plan
before you turn over.

Sally is just coming
down the garden path.
She is worried because
she cannot find her puppy, Flash.

Do you know where Flash is?
Look back at the plan.

He has gone round
to the side of the house
and is looking in
through the bedroom window.

key to plan

0   1 metre

Two centimetres
stand for one metre.

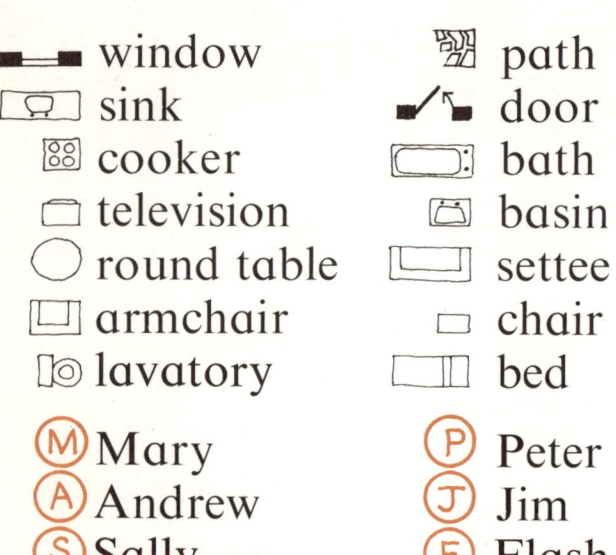

▬━▬ window	🌀 path
sink	door
cooker	bath
television	basin
○ round table	settee
armchair	chair
lavatory	bed

Ⓜ Mary   Ⓟ Peter

Ⓐ Andrew   Ⓙ Jim

Ⓢ Sally   Ⓕ Flash

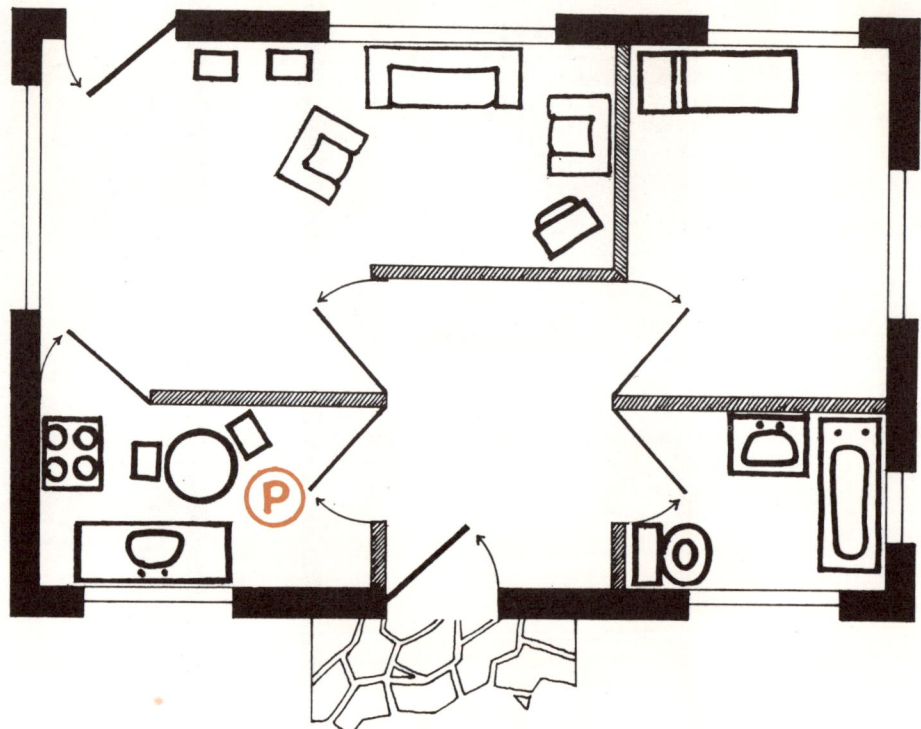

Here is the house again,
an hour later.

Can you see any changes?

We have moved some furniture.

Peter is finishing his lemonade.
Where have the other children
and Flash gone?

Now we can see
where they have gone.

We could not see them before
because our plan only showed
the house.
What we need is—

a plan of the house and garden.

key to plan

|————|
0   1 metre
One centimetre
stands for one metre.

hedge		fence	
rabbit hutch		bird table	
swing		flower bed	
goldfish pond		tree	
window		path	
sink		door	
cooker		bath	
television		basin	
round table		settee	
armchair		chair	
lavatory		bed	
(M) Mary		(P) Peter	
(A) Andrew		(J) Jim	
(S) Sally		(F) Flash	

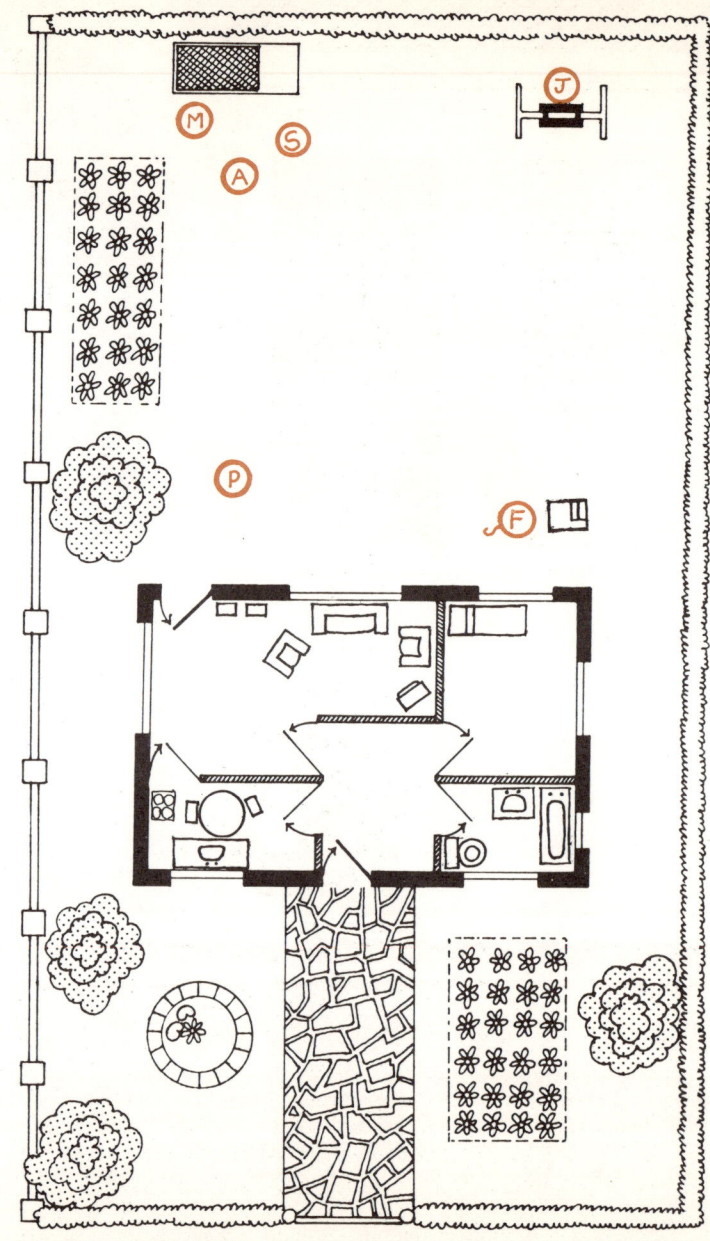

26

This plan has a different scale.
Because we wanted to show the
house *and* the garden,
we had to change the scale.
What is the scale now?
How long is the garden?
How wide is it?
How many flower beds are there?
How many trees?
Who is looking at the rabbit?
Where is Jim?

Flash finds the bird table
is more interesting.

key to plan

0 1 metre

One centimetre
stands for one metre.

hedge		fence	
rabbit hutch		bird table	
swing		flower bed	
goldfish pond		tree	
window		path	
sink		door	
cooker		bath	
television		basin	
round table		settee	
armchair		chair	
lavatory		bed	
M Mary		P Peter	
A Andrew		J Jim	
S Sally		F Flash	

Here is the plan of the house
and garden a little later on.

28

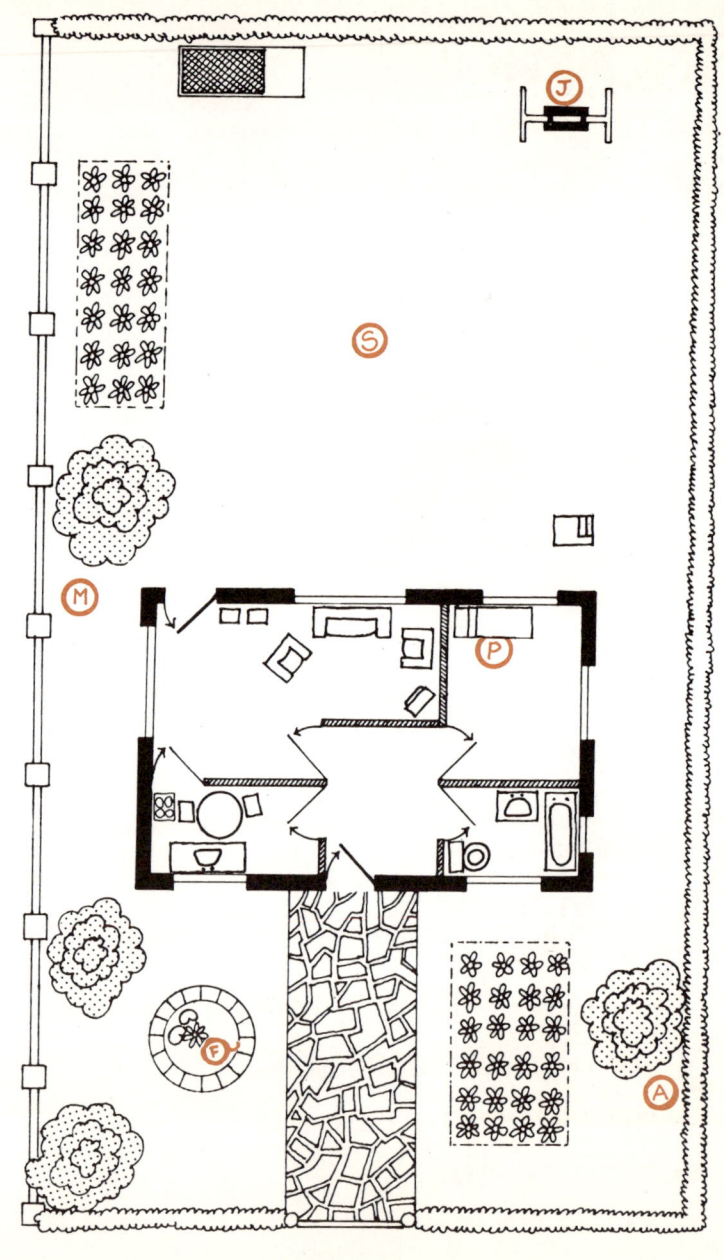

Now the children
are playing a game.
Can you guess what it is?

Who is the seeker?
Who is hiding under the bed?
Where are Andrew and Mary?
Who will be found first?

Where would you hide
if you were playing?

key to plan

0   1 metre

One centimetre
stands for one metre.

hedge		fence	
rabbit hutch		bird table	
swing		flower bed	
goldfish pond		tree	
window		path	
sink		door	
cooker		bath	
television		basin	
round table		settee	
armchair		chair	
lavatory		bed	
Ⓜ Mary		Ⓟ Peter	
Ⓐ Andrew		Ⓙ Jim	
Ⓢ Sally		Ⓕ Flash	

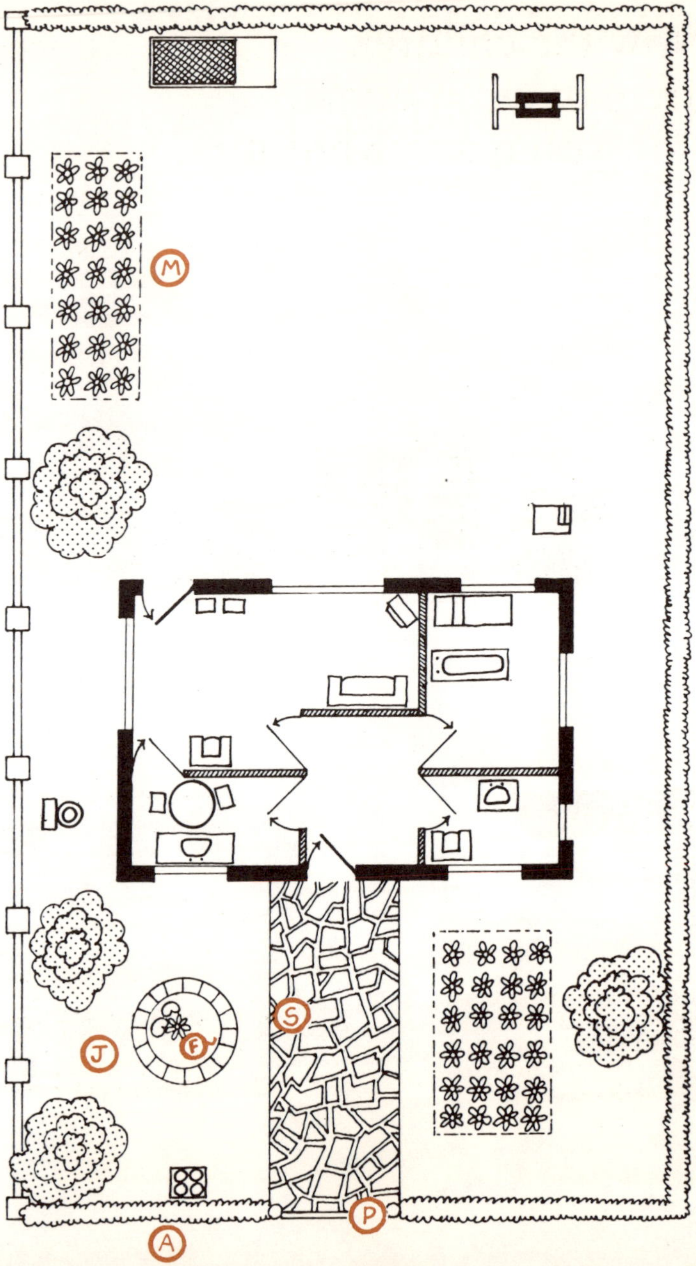

Now we have finished playing.
The children are going home.

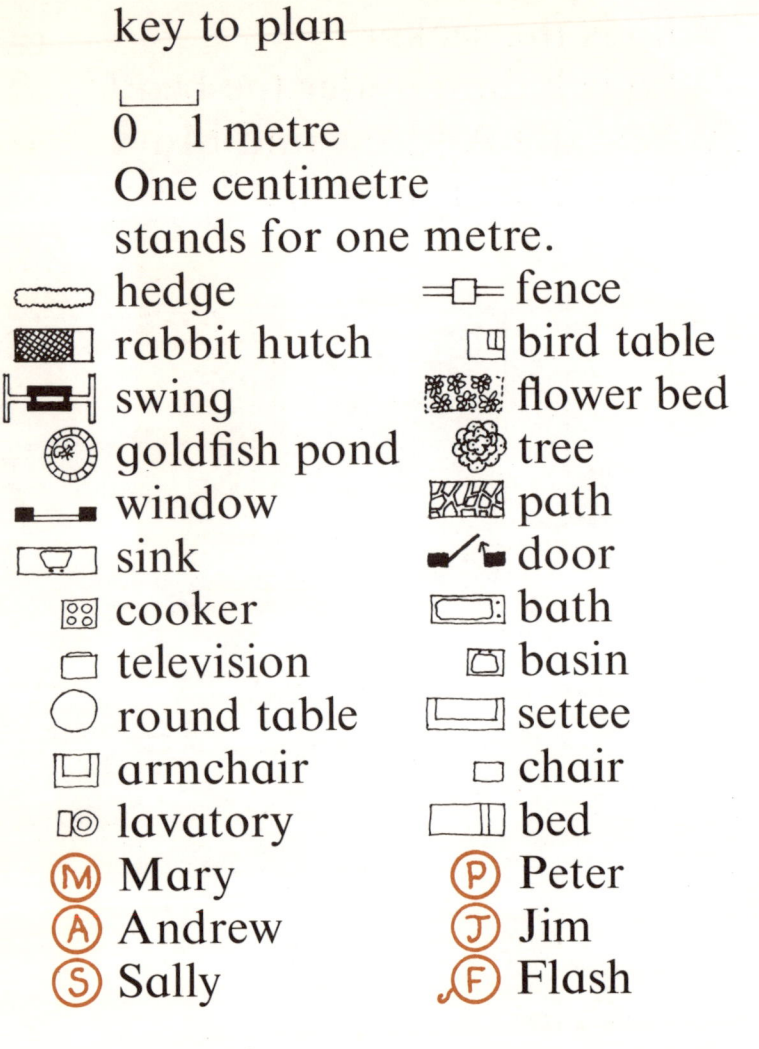

Who is the first to leave?
Is Flash following Sally?
Where is Peter?
Who is saying goodbye to the rabbit?
But—

who has moved
all the furniture around?

Puzzles

Look at page 24.
Can you see the pond
in the picture of the garden?
Why not?

Look at page 26.
Which of the children is nearest
to the bird table?

Look at page 28.
One person does not want to play
hide-and-seek.
Who is it?
Where is Flash?
How many doors must Peter go through
to get to the bathroom?
Can Sally find Flash without going
through the house?